THE 20TH CENTURY
Intermediate Level

25 Pieces by Barber, Bartók, Kabalevsky, Khachaturian,
Prokofiev, Ravel, Shostakovich and Others
in Progressive Order

Compiled and Edited by Richard Walters

T0066599

On the cover:
Castle and Sun (1928)
by Paul Klee (1879–1940)
Bridgeman Images
© 2015 Artists Rights Society (ARS), New York

ISBN 978-1-4950-1024-8

G. SCHIRMER, Inc.

DISTRIBUTED BY

HAL•LEONARD®
7777 W. BLUEMOUND RD. P.O. BOX 13819 MILWAUKEE, WI 53213

www.halleonard.com

CONTENTS

Though the table of contents appears in alphabetical order by composer, the music in this book is in progressive order.

COMPOSER BIOGRAPHIES, HISTORICAL NOTES
AND
PRACTICE AND PERFORMANCE TIPS

The pieces in this collection are by some of the greatest composers of the 20th century, composers who wrote a full range of music for orchestra, voices, piano, and chamber ensembles, in the great and large forms. But they also valued music education, and composed interesting music to foster a student pianist's progress. The music by these composers leads a student not only to technical proficiency, but also to become a more fully formed, imaginative musician. Some of these pieces challenge a student to broaden experience beyond conventional, traditional harmony and rhythm. In these works a piano student gets a glimpse into the mind of a great, forward-thinking artistic genius.

In the 20th century composers generally conceived every detail in a composition (unless it is left to chance by design). Many students do not seem to understand the organic role that slurs, phrases, staccatos, accents, dynamics, pedaling, and changes of tempo play in a 20th century composition. Tempo, articulation and dynamics are in mind from the outset of composition, as essential to the music as are the notes and rhythms.

In earlier centuries it was not the custom for the composer to necessarily notate all articulation and pedaling. Insightful understanding of period style of playing informs many of these details in music from the Baroque and Classical eras. Even in music of the 19th century composers did not always notate all such details, and a player's understanding of style is necessary in adding things implied but not stated in the score. Most composers of the 20th century became much more specific about notating such matters. Almost without exception, articulations and dynamics are not editorial suggestions in The 20th Century series. They are by the composer and part of the composition. If

editorial suggestions are very occasionally made, they are specifically noted on a piece or indicated in brackets.

Pedaling in The 20th Century series is by the composer unless indicated otherwise on an individual piece. Fingering is also often by the composer. Metronome indications without brackets are by the composer. In works where the composer did not provide a suggested metronome indication, those in brackets are editorial suggestions.

The "Practice and Performance Tips" point out a few ideas that may be helpful to the student in learning a piece. These might also be used by a busy teacher as an at-a-glance look at some topics in teaching a piece.

The pieces as part of sets for "children" are actually for progressing pianists of any age. Composers needed a way to indicate to the world that the pieces were written for a contained level of difficulty and for students, and were to be thought of differently from concert works such as a sonata or concerto, for example. The tradition of titling these with some variation along the lines of a "children's album" was a convenient way of solving this. It has always been understood, and certainly by the composers themselves, that this music is about the level of the pianist, not the age of the pianist.

When a great talent turns attention to writing a short piece of limited difficulty level for students, it is approached with the same aesthetics, temperament, tastes and creative invention applied when composing a symphony, opera or concerto. These exquisite miniatures are complete works of timeless art. Through them a master musician of the past indirectly teaches a progressing musician of the present and the future.

GEORGE ANTHEIL
(1900–1959, American)

After studying with Constantin von Sternberg in Philadelphia and Ernest Bloch in New York, American composer George Antheil moved to Berlin in 1922. He travelled around Europe as a concert pianist, often performing his own works. In 1923 he moved to Paris, where he became a prominent member of the avant-garde, befriending James Joyce, Ezra Pound, W.B. Yeats, Erik Satie and Pablo Picasso. His most famous piece is *Ballet mécanique* (1925), scored for multiple pianos, player pianos, percussion, siren, and two propellers. Due to the difficulty of executing a piece of such magnitude, it is known more theoretically than for actual performance. Antheil's earlier works, such as the *Ballet mécanique*, were often jazz-inspired, experimental and jarringly mechanistic. In the 1940s, back in the United States, Antheil turned to a more conventional style. A virtuoso concert pianist, he composed more for piano than any other instrument.

Little Shimmy (composed 1923)
"Little Shimmy" was composed in the same year as Antheil's professional debut as a concert pianist (at the Théâtre des Champs-Elysées in Paris), and Antheil may have played it on this recital, a great success attended by his illustrious supporters, such as James Joyce, Erik Satie, Ezra Pound, Jean Cocteau and Darius Milhaud. Classical composers in the U.S., as well as in Paris and Berlin, were discovering American jazz and blues in this period and incorporating those sounds into classical compositions. "Little Shimmy" is an example of just such a piece by a young American composer living in Paris.

Practice and Performance Tips
- Antheil indicated neither tempo nor dynamics. Editorial suggestions are in brackets.
- This fun piece relies on a relentlessly steady rhythm in the left hand.
- The following tricky measures require special practice, with attention to fingering: measures 3, 11, 13, 15, 21.
- The dotted eighth-note/sixteenth-note combination is like a "swing beat."
- Note that the deliberately insistent and shrill high treble diads in measures 12 and 14 are straight eighth notes, not swing beat.
- The parallel grace notes in the right and left hands in measures 8 and 18 need to be played both clearly and gracefully.
- Do not use any sustaining pedal, which would destroy the unsentimental joy of this carefree piece.

SAMUEL BARBER
(1910–1981, American)

Born in Pennsylvania, Samuel Barber was a precocious musical talent who composed from an early age, and at fourteen began studies in singing, piano, and composition at the Curtis Institute. One of the most prominent American composers of the 20th century, he is remembered for his distinctive neo-Romantic style. Early in his career he performed as a singer, which may have helped him develop an aptitude for writing the soaring melodic lines that define his works. Barber wrote for orchestra, voice, choir, piano, chamber ensemble, and solo instruments and was well acclaimed during his lifetime. After 1938, almost all of his compositions were written on commission from renowned performers and ensembles. Among his well-known pieces are the *Adagio for Strings* (1936), the opera *Vanessa* (1956–57), *Knoxville: Summer of 1915* (1947), and *Hermit Songs* (1953).

Petite Berceuse (composed c. 1923)
This piece by the thirteen year old Samuel Barber showed marked progress in his compositions. It remained unpublished in his lifetime. It was first published in *Samuel Barber: Early Piano Works* (2010), and also included in *Samuel Barber: Complete Piano Music, Revised Edition*.

Practice and Performance Tips
- This lovely, lyrical piece is about a melody in the right hand, with a simple accompaniment in the left hand.
- Notice Barber's marking of *dolce semplice* (sweet and simply).
- Barber's music in general, including this piece, is about a strong sense of melodic phrase.
- Play the sixteenth notes in measures 8 and 15 gently; this is not about a showy display
- The dynamic arch of the piece is paramount. The *ff* climax in measure 27 is followed by a quick diminuendo to *p*.
- The return of the melody in the final section (beginning in measure 31) played *pp* is a lovely, quiet recapitulation.
- There is some *rubato* (slight relaxing or surging of tempo) implied in this romantic piece, although the composer has written most of this in (measures 8–9, 15–17, 26–32). However, keep it simple (*dolce semplice*) and do not play with too much sentiment.
- This music needs careful pedaling. Note the editorial suggestions for this.

To My Steinway from *Three Sketches for Pianoforte*
(composed 1923–24)
Barber's father published *Three Sketches for Pianoforte* in a private, very limited edition in 1924, but in practical terms they remained unpublished and unavailable in the composer's lifetime. The set was posthumously published in *Samuel Barber: Early Piano Works* (2010), and also included in *Samuel Barber: Complete Piano Music, Revised Edition.*

"To My Steinway" is the second piece in the set, composed in June of 1923, when Barber was thirteen years old. It is dedicated "to Number 230601," the manufacturing number on the Steinway piano that his parents had given him. Barber's love for the piano, and for piano literature the piece echoes, is obvious.

Practice and Performance Tips
- This tender music needs to be played lovingly.
- It is a song-like piece, with the melody (on top) predominant.
- Many student pianists will need to practice the rolled chords.
- Context determines how fast or slow a chord should be rolled. In this Adagio piece, do not roll the chords too quickly.
- Think of these rolled chords as a beautiful harmony to be savored, emerging from the lowest note to the top note.

BÉLA BARTÓK

(1881–1945, Hungarian; became a US citizen in 1945)

Béla Bartók is one of the most important and often performed composers of the twentieth century, and much of his music, including *Concerto for Orchestra*, his concertos, his string quartets, and his opera *Bluebeard's Castle*, holds a venerable position in the classical repertoire. His parents were amateur musicians who nurtured their young son with exposure to dance music, drumming, and piano lessons. In 1899 he started piano and composition studies at the Academy of Music in Budapest and not long after graduation he joined the Academy's piano faculty. Bartók wished to create music that was truly Hungarian at its core, a desire that sparked his deep interest in folk music. His work collecting and studying folksongs from around the Baltic region impacted his own compositional style greatly in terms of rhythm, mood, and texture. Bartók utilized folk influences to create a truly unique style. Though he composed opera, concertos, ballets, and chamber music, he was also committed to music education and composed several piano works for students, including his method *Mikrokosmos*. Bartók toured extensively in the 1920s and '30s, and became as well-known as both a pianist and composer. He immigrated to the US in 1940 to escape war and political turmoil in Europe, and settled in New York City, though the last years of his life were difficult, with many health problems.

Bagatelle No. 6 from *Fourteen Bagatelles*, Sz. 38, BB 50 (composed 1908)
Bartók stated the following about the *Fourteen Bagatelles* of 1908. "In these, a new piano style appears as a reaction to the exuberance of the romantic piano music of the nineteenth century, a style stripped of all unessential decorative elements, using only the most restricted technical means. As later developments show, the *Bagatelles* inaugurate a new trend of piano writing in my career, which is consistently followed in almost all of my successive piano works."

Practice and Performance Tips
- This pensive Bagatelle is an excellent introduction to Bartók's lyrical modernism, an individual style which was forming in the early twentieth century.
- Though the notes are not difficult to master, the piece needs insightful and intelligent phrasing and musicality.
- Practice the melodic phrases (such as right hand measures 1–2, or 3–4; or left hand measures 8–9) with very *legato* fingers.
- You must pay careful attention to all Bartók's details of dynamics, decrescendos, accents, diminuendo.
- It this piece is played without understanding the composer's carefully written sense of phrase, it runs the risk of sounding like a rather random succession of notes.
- Practice without pedal. However, very light touches of pedal might be applied judiciously in performance.

Selections from *For Children*, Sz. 42, BB 53
(composed 1908–09)
Bartók was one of the pioneering ethnomusicologists in eastern Europe, collecting and documenting thousands of folksongs from Hungary and neighboring countries. The original edition of *For Children* was in four volumes. Volumes 1–2 were compositions based on Hungarian folk songs. Volumes 3–4 were compositions based on Slovakian folk songs. Bartók created a revised edition in 1943, with only minor changes to the original regarding compositional content, with the pieces retitled. Some pieces were eliminated for the revised edition, and the four volumes were consolidated into two. In the preface to *For Children* Bartók wrote that the pieces were designed to teach young players "the simple and non-Romantic beauties of folk music."

Jeering Song (Volume 1)
From Volume 2 in the original four volume edition, with the English title "Wedding Day." Bartók changed the title for the revised edition.

Practice and Performance Tips

- The piece is about crisp and insistent rhythm.
- It has the irregular phrase structure typical of an Eastern European folk dance.
- Practice in sections. Section 1: measures 1–12; Section 2: measures 13–22; Section 3: measures 23–37.
- In Section 1 play with staccato, noting the accented downbeats of most measures.
- When the melody of Section 1 returns for Section 3 notice how Bartók placed different accents, stressing beat 2 rather than beat 1 the second time. This adds playfulness to the "jeering."
- Practice left hand alone in measures 13–20, playing staccato and evenly.
- Bartók has added possible grace notes in the *ossia* (optional). Attempt to play these, practicing separately. If you cannot manage the grace notes with the chords, simply leave them out and play the section without the grace notes. Bartók surely knew that these grace notes would be problematic for some student pianists.
- Carefully observe the dynamics the composer has written, which feature sharp contrasts.
- The music should be very steady, with no fluctuation in tempo.
- Use no sustaining pedal until the end, where an editorial suggestion is notated.

Round Dance (Volume 1)

From Volume 1 in the original four volume edition, with the English title "The Girl in White." Bartók changed the title for the revised edition.

Practice and Performance Tips

- Practice the right-hand folk melody separately, paying close attention to the composer's slurs and dynamics.
- Shape the right-hand melody expressively, but maintain steadiness.
- Practice the left hand separately, using the composer's pedaling.
- Notice that Bartók intends that the pedal is cleared after the second left-hand chord is played in measures 1–7.
- The very specific pedaling stated above helps create the phrasing in each measure.
- Bartók *does not* intend that the pedal should be held through beats 3 and 4 and change on beat 1 of the next measure in measures 1–7. This would create a bland performance.
- Though it is Lento, Bartók's indication of quarter note = 70 doesn't feel extremely slow.
- Keep a steady beat throughout until the last measure, when a *slight ritardando* is possible.

PAUL CRESTON
(1906–1985, American)

Paul Creston was born into a poor Italian immigrant family in New York. As a child he took piano and organ lessons but was self-taught in theory and composition. In 1938 Creston was awarded a Guggenheim Fellowship, and in 1941 the New York Music Critics' Circle Award. He served as the director of A.S.C.A.P. from 1960–1968, and was composer-in-residence and professor of music at Central Washington State College from 1968–1975. His works, which include additions to orchestral, vocal, piano, and chamber music repertoire, often feature shifting rhythmic patterns. He wrote a number of solos for instruments customarily left out of the limelight, such as the marimba, accordion, or saxophone. Creston was an important composition teacher (John Corigliano studied with him), and also wrote the books *Principles of Rhythm* and *Rational Metric Notation*.

Selections from *Five Little Dances*, Op. 24
(composed 1940)

Rustic Dance, Op. 24, No. 1
Practice and Performance Tips

- Begin practice slowly hands separately.
- Learn the articulations (accents, staccato) as you learn the notes and rhythms.
- Divide the piece into sections for your practice. For instance: Section 1: measures 1–12; Section 2: measures 13–24; Section 3: measures 25–34; Section 4: measures 35–46.
- Notice how the texture changes from accented, loud and *non legato* to smooth and soft in measure 13.
- When you can play each hand separately accurately, move to practicing hands together at a slow tempo.
- Continue to observe the articulations you learned when practicing hands separately.
- Pay careful attention to the dynamics the composer has written.
- Do not take this piece too quickly as a performance tempo.
- Keep the tempo absolutely steady.
- Note the composer's marking "Heavily" and the title "Rustic Dance" in finding the character of the music.

Festive Dance, Op. 24, No. 5
Practice and Performance Tips

- Begin practice slowly hands separately.
- Pay careful attention in practicing the left hand alone, noting the composer's marking of both *strongly rhythmic* and *legato*.
- It is paramount that the left hand remains steady and even throughout.
- In practicing the right hand alone, attempt to move smoothly from chord to chord.

8

- Note the accents the composer has marked.
- For practice it helps to divide a piece such as this into sections. For instance, Section 1: measures 1–8; Section 2: measures 9–20; Section 3: measures 21–26; Section 4: measures 27–32; Section 5: measures 33–45.
- Sharp dynamic contrasts (from *f* to a sudden *p*, for instance) are part of the character of the music.
- The composer has indicated dotted quarter note = 96. It's possible to take the piece at a quicker pace, but be careful not to take it too quickly.
- Use no sustaining pedal throughout.

ALAN HOVHANESS
(1911–2000, American)

Alan Hovhaness was born in Somerville, Massachusetts, and studied at the New England Conservatory with Frederick Converse. He became interested in the music of India, to which he was exposed by musicians in the Boston area, and later looked to his Armenian heritage as well as music from Japan and Korea for inspiration. A prolific composer, Hovhaness' over five hundred works include all the major genres of western art music. He wrote six ballets as well as other stage works, sixty-six symphonies, works for chorus and voice, and numerous chamber and piano pieces. One of his most well-known works is his Symphony No. 2 *Mysterious Mountain*, premiered by Leopold Stokowski and the Philadelphia Orchestra in 1955. His career went through a number of stages, incorporating aspects from the Renaissance and the Romantic era in addition to traditions outside Western classical music. Despite these shifts in style, he consistently sought to portray a connection between music, spirituality, and nature. Mountains particularly moved him, and he chose to live much of his life in Switzerland and the Pacific Northwest due to the proximity of these regions to the landscape that served as his muse.

Mountain Lullaby from *Mountain Idylls*, Op. 119, No. 3 (composed 1931, 1949, 1955)
This set was subtitled "Three Easy Pieces for Piano." Published as set in 1955, the three pieces were written at various times. An idyll is a poem describing a pastoral, simple scene. Hovhaness was particularly fond of mountains.

Practice and Performance Tips
- Chromaticism and dissonance is part of twentieth century style. Learn to appreciate the unique colors of the harmonies.
- In chromatic music you must be absolutely sure that you are playing the right notes. Check very carefully.
- Throughout, the right hand is playing a haunting melody over the left-hand chords.
- The composer has written very specific pedaling

that must be explicitly observed for the character of this quietly mysterious piece to emerge.
- It may help to conjure an image to create a performance, such as something barely visible in the mountain mist at twilight.
- Largo, with quarter note = about 40 is the composer's marking. Until you learn the piece very well, it will be difficult to convincingly sustain this music at this slow tempo.

DMITRI KABALEVSKY
(1904–1987, Russian)

Kabalevsky was an important Russian composer of the Soviet era who wrote music in many genres, including four symphonies, a handful of operas, theatre and film scores, patriotic music, choral music, vocal music, and numerous piano works. He embraced the Soviet notion of socialist realism in art, a fact that was more than politically advantageous to his career in the USSR. While studying piano and composition at the Moscow Conservatory, he taught piano lessons at a music college and it was for these students that he began writing works for young players. In 1932 he began teaching at the Moscow Conservatory, earning the title of professor in 1939. He eventually went on to develop programs for the concert hall, radio, and television aimed at teaching children about classical music. In the last decades of his life, Kabalevsky focused on developing music curricula for schools, retiring from the Moscow Conservatory to teach in public schools where he could test his theories and the effectiveness of his syllabi. This he considered his true life's work, and his pedagogical principles revolutionized music education in Russia. A collection of his writings on music education was published in English in 1988 as *Music and Education: A Composer Writes About Musical Education*.

Selections from *30 Pieces for Children*, Op. 27
(composed 1937–38)
Kabalevsky often quoted Maxim Gorki, saying that books for children should be "the same as for adults, only better." Kabalevsky believed strongly in writing music for young players that was not dumbed-down, but rather, complete, imaginative compositions unto themselves. Kabalevsky did a slight revision of Op. 27 in 1985, which was intended to be an authoritative edition. (This is our source for the pieces in this collection.)

Clowning, Op. 27, No. 10
Practice and Performance Tips
- Kabalevsky was a master at writing pieces for students that sound brilliant without being impossibly difficult.
- There would be no point to practicing this piece hands separately. Practice hands together, slowly at first.

- Notice the articulation pattern almost throughout: a staccato eighth note in the left hand answered by two slurred eighth notes in the right hand.
- Aim for evenness and steadiness in the eighth notes, and clarity of touch and articulation.
- Kabalevsky asks for a tenuto stress and pedaling on the dotted half note at the end of a phrase, ending the phrase with a different tone color.
- Dynamic contrasts are very clear and should be crisply observed.
- Notice the soft pedal (*una corda*) in measures 25–32, and again in 43–44, which will also give a different tone color.
- Use no sustaining pedal except where indicated.
- As you master the piece, gradually increase your practice tempo, always keeping a steady beat whatever the tempo.
- The texture of this music requires a buoyant touch, even in *f* sections.

A Little Prank, Op. 27, No. 13
Practice and Performance Tips
- The title indicates playfulness, and the composer gives unexpected twists in the harmony.
- Divide the piece into three sections for practice. Section 1: measures 1–16; Section 2: pickup to measure 17–33; Section 3: measures 34–53.
- Begin practice slowly, hands together.
- The descending five-finger scales in the right hand need to be played with crystal clear evenness.
- Note the composer's marking of *leggiero*, which means lightly.
- The music relies on its articulation; note the slurring and staccato markings.
- Use absolutely no sustaining pedal.
- Most students will need to give measures 20–22 and 28–30 special attention. Practice these hands separately, then hands together slowly.
- Gradually increase your practice tempo over time, but always keeping a steady beat.

Lyric Piece, Op. 27, No. 16
Practice and Performance Tips
- As might be guessed of music titled "Lyric Piece," it is primarily about song-like melody.
- The right-hand melody should predominate over the left-hand accompaniment in measures 3–12.
- The melody moves to the left hand in measures 12–17, before returning to the right hand in measure 17.
- Practice the melody, noted above, separately, aiming to create a smooth and musically pleasing line, using the phrasing that Kabalevsky has composed to shape the melody.
- The melancholy spirit, combined with the long melody, is reminiscent of Chopin.
- Pedaling is explicitly marked by the composer. Practice the left hand alone with the pedaling.

- The composer takes the music into unexpected harmony in measure 17, then again in measure 21.
- Except for the opening motive, which returns at the end of measure 31, this is quiet music, marked *p*. Do not allow it to bloom too far past that quiet dynamic.

The Chase, Op. 27, No. 21
Practice and Performance Tips
- This piece, with hands in octaves throughout, creates a brilliant and exciting impact.
- When well played it sounds harder than it actually is, because the music lies so easily under the hands.
- Divide the piece into sections and practice slowly hands and separately.
- For instance practice measures 1–8 first with right hand only, then left hand only.
- Continue throughout the piece in sections with this approach.
- Left-hand agility is the challenge for most student pianists.
- When putting hands together, only play as quickly as the left hand has mastered the music.
- From the very beginning of practice pay attention to slurs, staccato and accents.
- Learning the articulation from the start will help you learn the notes and rhythms.
- Kabalevsky would have written in pedaling had he intended it. Use no pedal.

Novelette, Op. 27, No. 25
Practice and Performance Tips
- The title "Novelette" was originally invented by Schumann (his Op. 21) for pensive, solemn music that tells a melancholy story.
- Over the left-hand fifths, the right hand plays a melody that is almost always doubled in thirds.
- In the right hand use *legato* fingers to create the phrases and slurs the composers has written.
- The left hand moves up chromatically from measure 24 to the climax (and loudest) point of the piece in measure 38.
- Pedal carefully. Kabalevsky intends that the sustaining pedal should be changed on each downbeat.

Slow Waltz from *24 Pieces for Children*, Op. 39, No. 23 (composed 1944)
Kabalevsky began writing piano music for students as early as 1927. His first major set, *30 Children's Pieces* of Op. 27, was composed in 1937–38. The *24 Pieces for Children* (alternately titled *24 Easy Pieces*) of Op. 39 is for an earlier level of study than Op. 27. Though Kabalevsky composed operas, orchestral music, concertos and chamber music throughout his career, as well as more difficult piano literature, he returned to writing music for piano students periodically in his life, reflecting his deeply felt commitment to music education.

Practice and Performance Tips
- The piece echoes the spirit of a simple, melancholy waltz by Chopin.
- Begin practice slowly with hands separately.
- The challenge is to gracefully and deftly move the left hand position on the keyboard, as it moves around in staccato playing, in measures 1–8, and measures 25–32.
- Notice how the piece is composed to allow *più mosso* (more movement, or a little faster) in measures 8–24, with the hand positions not jumping around in the left hand in this section.
- Pay careful attention to all slurs, staccatos, stresses and dynamics.
- Notice the longer melody phrases the middle section, measures 8–24.
- Kabalevsky intended the piece to be played without sustaining pedal. Use no pedal.
- With no sustaining pedal to hide behind, clarity in all details become very exposed.

Rondo-Toccata from *Four Rondos*, Op. 60, No. 4
(composed 1958)
Practice and Performance Tips
- The piece can create a brilliant impact in performance. Because the left hand remains in a contained position through much of it, it will sound more difficult than it is.
- Practice hands separately, slowly at first.
- Learn the articulation (staccato touch) from the beginning.
- Use the sustaining pedal only where explicitly indicated by Kabalevsky.
- Note the change of touch, moving from staccato to legato in measure 17.
- With the hands playing the same notes in octaves beginning in measure 19, make sure both right and left hands are playing exactly the same articulation.
- Practice tempo can increase as you master the music, but always maintain steadiness.
- Only play the piece as fast as you can manage in making it sound under control. Do not let it run away from you.

Prelude and Fugue in G Major
from *Six Preludes and Fugues*, Op. 61, No. 1
(composed 1958–59)
Practice and Performance Tips
- Play the Prelude section with the care of a chorale, with rounded tone and with the top treble note only slightly brought out.
- Make sure all the notes of the chords sound exactly together in the Prelude, and the harmonies are clear.
- Tasteful use of the sustaining pedal is needed for the Prelude (and its reprise at the end). Make sure you carefully pedal to clarify the change of harmony.
- The Fugue begins in measure 21.

- Practice each hand separately in the Fugue.
- Use no sustaining pedal in the Fugue.
- This Fugue should be played very evenly and cleanly, in the spirit of a Baroque fugue.
- The trickiest spot comes with the crossing of the hands in measures 48–49. Prepare for this.
- Your tempo for the Fugue should be determined by the tempo at which you can manage measures 48–49 gracefully.

ARAM KHACHATURIAN
(1903–1978, Soviet/Armenian)

Aram Khachaturian was a seminal figure in 20th century Armenian and Soviet culture. Beloved in his homeland for bringing Armenia to prominence within the realm of Western art music, a major concert hall in Armenia's capital Yerevan bears his name, as well as a string quartet and an international competition for piano and composition. Born in Tbilisi, Georgia, of Armenian heritage, he grew up listening to Armenian folk songs but was also exposed to classical music early on through the Tbilisi's chapter of the Russian Music Society, the city's Italian Opera Theater, and visits by musicians such as Sergei Rachmaninoff. He moved to Moscow to study composition in 1921. Khachaturian's musical language combined folk influences with the Russian romantic tradition, embodying the official Soviet arts policy. He used traditional forms, such as theme and variations, sonata form, and Baroque suite forms, in creative ways, juxtaposing them with Armenian melodies and religious songs, folk dance rhythms, and a harmonic language that took inspiration from folk instruments such as the saz. He wrote symphonies, instrumental concertos, sonatas, ballets, and was the first Armenian composer to write film music. Khachaturian's most recognizable composition to the general public is "Sabre Dance" from the ballet *Gayane*. Starting in 1950, he also became active as an internationally touring conductor. He was awarded the Order of Lenin in 1939 and the Hero of Socialist Labor in 1973.

Ivan Sings from *Adventures of Ivan*
(composition begun 1926, completed 1947)
Khachaturian composed two Albums for Children. The first, completed in 1947, included *Adventures of Ivan*.

Practice and Performance Tips
- The right hand is the singing (*cantabile*), rather sad melody throughout; the left hand is an accompaniment to this melody.
- Practice the right-hand melody separately, making it expressive in the way the composer intends, using the dynamics, crescendos, decrescendos, and slurs.
- The left hand also needs practice separately.

- Play the repeated quarter note diads in the left hand very evenly.
- Practice the pedal Khachaturian has composed, applying it very specifically when practicing left hand alone.
- Except for the spots marked *rit.* (measures 16–17 and 28) and *poco sostenuto* (measures 26–27), the beat should be played steadily throughout.

ROBERT MUCZYNSKI

(1929–2010, American)

Composer and pianist Robert Muczynski studied at DePaul University in his hometown of Chicago with Alexander Tcherepnin. A brilliant pianist, at twenty-nine he made his Carnegie Hall debut with a performance of his own compositions. In addition to solo piano works, Muczynski mainly wrote for small chamber ensembles and also composed several orchestral pieces. His flute and saxophone sonatas, as well as *Time Pieces* for clarinet and piano, have become part of the standard repertoire for those instruments. In 1981, his concerto for saxophone was nominated for the Pulitzer Prize. Muczynski was composer in residence on the faculty of the University of Arizona from 1965 until his retirement in 1988.

Fable No. 9 from *Fables*, Op. 21 (composed 1965)
This set is subtitled "Nine Pieces for the Young," and was written for an eight-year-old piano student. Each of the fables has a distinct character. Muczynski was an excellent pianist, and his understanding of the instrument is evident in these compositions. About *Fables* the composer stated, "Few people realize how difficult it is to compose a piece that stays within the restrictions of that level. You have to restrain yourself when it comes to key choice, rhythmic complexity, and range. In *Fables* I tried to use strong patterns with the idea of liberating one hand by assigning it a repeating rhythmic or melodic figure."[1]

[1]From the preface to *Robert Muczynski: Collected Piano Pieces*, G. Schirmer, 1990.

Practice and Performance Tips
- Begin practice slowly hands separately, retaining a steady eighth note beat.
- You may divide your practice into three sections. Section 1: measures 1–8; Section 2: measures 9–18; Section 3: measures 19–29.
- In Sections 1 and 3 pay careful attention to the composer's accents, slurs and staccato markings in the right hand. These will help propel the insistent rhythm.
- In Sections 1 and 3 the left-hand eighth notes must be absolutely steady.
- Move to practicing hands together, first at a slow tempo, but retaining a steady beat.

- In Section 2 the left hand plays legato, the right-hand chords are essentially staccato.
- The return of the opening material (measure 19) is *p*, with a sudden burst of *f* in measure 23.
- The composer's metronome indication of a full 5/8 measure = 52 is extremely fast. If you cannot attain this, play at the fastest tempo you can manage, keeping a very steady beat throughout.
- Use no pedal at all until the composer's pedal marking on the final chord.

OCTAVIO PINTO

(1890–1950, Brazilian)

Octavio Pinto was born in Sao Paulo, Brazil, and enjoyed a successful career as an architect, but he was also an avid music lover, a skillful composer and pianist, and was well-connected to musical life in Brazil. In 1922 he married the famous piano virtuoso Gulomar Novaes, and he was also a close friend of composer Heitor Villa-Lobos. He took lessons for a time from Isidore Philipp, but it was mostly as a composer that his love and talent for music expressed itself throughout his life. He composed piano music, generally character pieces in nature or showpieces, until his death. His most well-known and oft-played work is *Scenas Infantis* (Memories of Childhood) of 1932, which became a signature piece performed by Novaes.

Playing Marbles (Bolinhas de vidro) from *Children's Festival: Little Suite for the Piano* (composed 1939)
Practice and Performance Tips
- This music requires a light touch throughout to achieve the composer's indication of *staccatissimo*.
- Begin practice slowly hands separately, learning the articulation (primarily staccato, spelled by occasional slurs) from the beginning.
- Divide the music into sections for practice. Section 1: measures 1 through beat 1 of measure 13; Section 2: beat 2 of measure 13 through beat 1 of measure 21; Section 3: beat 2 of measure 21 through beat 1 of measure 27; Section 4: beat 2 of measure 27 to the end.
- Section by section, after hands alone practice, practice hands together, first at a slow tempo, retaining the staccatos and slurs.
- Alternating fingers on repeated notes (measures 5–6, 13–14, 17–20) is classic piano technique. After practicing this and mastering it, you will realize that it produces a buoyant and even sound that playing these repeated notes with one finger will never match.
- Practice the parallel fourth scales in measures 21–24 very carefully. Note that after beginning as chromatic scales they move to a typical major scale for the last two beats.

- Only increase your practice tempo when you have mastered the notes, rhythms and articulations.
- Do not attempt to play this piece faster than you can manage.
- No pedal at all until the composer's marking in measure 31.
- Many student pianists encountering this piece may never have played a glissando. With your right hand rolled away from you and turned upside down, rest the fingernail of the three finger on the B natural note where the glissando begins.
- Using your fingernail only, slide it over the white keys until you reach beat one of the next measure, and strike this note conventionally with the same finger. Be careful not to use the knuckle of your finger, as this can hurt and cause bleeding.

SERGEI PROKOFIEV
(1891–1953, Russian)

Russian composer and pianist Sergei Prokofiev pushed the boundaries of Russian Romanticism without fully disregarding its influence. Influenced by the formal aspects of works by Haydn and Mozart, he was also a pioneering neo-classicist. Prokofiev was born in eastern Ukraine, but travelled often with his mother to Moscow and St. Petersburg where he was exposed to works such as Gounod's *Faust*, Borodin's *Prince Igor*, Tchaikovsky's *Sleeping Beauty*, and operas such as *La Traviata* and *Carmen*. His prodigious musical abilities as a child led him to lessons with Reinhold Glière and then studies at the St. Petersburg Conservatory. He composed several sonatas and symphonies during his studies, as well as his first piano concerto, which he played for his piano exam at the conservatory, taking first prize. In 1917, following the October Revolution, he left Russia, first moving to the United States and then settling in Europe. He continued to tour internationally after returning to the Soviet Union in 1936, until the authorities confiscated his passport two years later. During World War II Prokofiev was evacuated from the Soviet Union. It was a difficult time for composers and artists in Soviet Russia. Between 1946 and '48, Soviet political leader Andrey Zhdanov passed a number of resolutions with the intent of heavily regulating artistic output and keeping it in line with the ideals of socialist realism and the Communist party.

Selections from *Music for Children*, Op. 65
(composed 1935)
In the midst of many months of work on the large ballet *Romeo and Juliet*, a commission from the Kirov Ballet, Prokofiev refreshed his creativity briefly by shifting his focus to composing the twelve piano miniatures comprising *Music for Children*, Op. 65.

Morning, Op. 65, No. 1
Practice and Performance Tips
- One of the implied topics that Prokofiev is teaching is the need for a graceful shift of hand position into different ranges of the piano, including the crossing of hands. These need to be anticipated and played with elegance or they will sound clumsy.
- Divide the piece into sections for practice. Section 1: measures 1–8; Section 2: measures 9–17; Section 3: measures 18–23; Section 4: measures 24–29.
- Though the music is full of colorful features and figures, it is contained in volume and quiet in spirit. It may help some pianists to first learn the piece playing at *mf*, then later apply the composer's dynamics of *p*, *mp*, *pp*, etc.
- Practice measures 9–17 right hand alone, playing with evenness and clarity.
- Bring out the left-hand melody in measures 9–17, playing with beautiful tone and legato phrasing.
- The hands trade at measure 18, with the eighth notes moving to the left hand. Practice left hand alone in this section, aiming for evenness and clarity.
- Play measure 23 very gracefully or the notes will sound "wrong."
- Apply tasteful use of the sustaining pedal.

Promenade, Op. 65, No. 2
Practice and Performance Tips
- The composer's implication for the left-hand quarter notes in measures 1–20 without articulation markings is that these should be played with slight separation. If he had intended legato playing, he would have indicated this.
- The above means that in spots such as measures 4 or 6, the right hand is playing a smooth legato and the left hand is playing slightly detached.
- Practice without any sustaining pedal. The entire piece would easily be played with no pedal. If you choose to add it in spots, use taste and care.
- Anticipate the crossing of hands to manage it gracefully, in measures 45–50.
- Do not take this *Allegretto* too quickly.

Regrets, Op. 65, No. 5
Practice and Performance Tips
- Prokofiev's ability to make such a strong emotional statement in such a brief piece reminds one of Schumann.
- The priorities are: tone, phrasing, dynamics, careful pedaling, and in general, sensitive musicality.
- Notice the specific notes that Prokofiev has marked with the stress or tenuto marking, and experiment in how to bring those notes out expressively.
- There are sharp and swift dynamic changes that need to be played deliberately, like bursts of emotion. For example, measures 4–5, measures 8–9, measures 28–29, measures 42–43.

- You must prepare for the hand crossing required and accomplish it gracefully: right hand crosses left in measures 7, 20, 32.
- The "hairpin" rise and fall in volume also imply some phrasing.
- Practice the middle section (measures 17–24) without pedal, aiming for clarity and evenness in the treble eighth notes of the right hand.
- Notice the "comma" (meaning a brief and graceful lift of the hands) at the end of measure 16 before moving to the *tranquillo* middle section.
- The composer decorates the melody with variations upon its return in measure 25.
- The surprising change of harmony and content at measure 37 is marked with *pp*, which can be magical. This piece needs the addition of sustaining pedal, but learn it without pedal first. Then apply it judiciously, and sparingly.
- Do not be afraid of expressing the emotion (the sharp, remorseful pain of regret, and the sadness that accompanies it) that the composer has created.

MAURICE RAVEL
(1875–1937, French)

Ravel is, along with Debussy, considered the most important French composer of the twentieth century. He was raised in Paris but born in Ciboure, a Basque villa in the southwestern corner of France to Swiss and Basque parents. His lifelong use of exotic influences in his music stemmed from his heritage-based affinity for Basque and Spanish culture. Ravel studied piano and then composition with Gabriel Fauré at the Paris Conservatoire, though he was dismissed for not meeting the necessary requirements in either piano or composition. This, along with his heritage, may have influenced the lack of support he received from French music critics and the Société Nationale de Musique, Paris' leading concert society. Critics often pitted him unfavorably against Debussy and accused him of copying Debussy's style. In 1909, Ravel founded the Société Musicale Indépendente in opposition to the Société Nationale, naming Fauré president. This society strove to organize performances of both French and foreign works regardless of their style or genre. The same year he wrote *Daphnis et Chloé* for famed choreographer Diaghilev and began his close friendship with Igor Stravinsky. He joined the army as a driver in the motor transport corps during World War I, a tragic time in which he was also deeply affected by the loss of his mother, with whom he was extremely close. He lived the rest of his life thirty miles west of Paris in Montfort-l'Amaury surrounded by the Forest of Rambouillet, travelling around Europe and North America performing and attending premieres of his works. Ravel is remembered as a supreme orchestrator. His

orchestration of Mussorgsky's *Pictures at an Exhibition* holds a place in standard orchestral repertoire, as does *Bolero*, his most famous piece and a textbook example of his skills in orchestration.

Prélude (composed 1913)
Practice and Performance Tips

- French style in the Impressionist period requires sophistication of touch, phrasing, pedaling and musicality.
- This piece is about elegant, languorous phrase and lush harmony.
- Play the eighth note figures throughout very smoothly.
- Pay careful attention to Ravel's phrase markings.
- The section measures 10–15 will require careful attention, as the hands are close together, with the right hand playing on top of the left hand.
- The rolled chord in the right hand in measure 16 and 18 will take some practice for most hands. If your hand is too small to hold all the notes down after they are rolled, then experiment with letting one or two of the notes go, sustaining the sound with careful use of the sustaining pedal.
- Pedal needs to be applied. Be careful to keep the harmonies clear. Do make this or any other Impressionist piece a vague blur of sound.

DMITRI SHOSTAKOVICH
(1906–1975, Russian)

A major mid-twentieth century composer, Shostakovich is famous for his epic symphonies, concertos, operas, string quartets, and other chamber works. Born in St. Petersburg, his entire career took place in Soviet-era Russia. His life teetered between receiving high official honors and living with an almost debilitating fear of arrest for works that did not adhere to the Soviet ideals of socialist realism. In 1934, his opera *Lady Macbeth of the Mtsensk District* met with great popular success, but was banned by Stalin for the next thirty years as modernist, surrealist, and obscene. The following year, Stalin began a campaign known as the Purges, executing or exiling to prison camps politicians, intellectuals and artists. Shostakovich managed to avoid such a fate, and despite an atmosphere of anxiety and repression was able to compose an astounding number of works with originality, humor, and emotional power. He succeeded in striking a balance between modernism and tradition that continues to make his music accessible to a broad audience. An excellent pianist, Shostakovich performed concertos by Mozart, Prokofiev, and Tchaikovsky early in his career, but after 1930 limited himself to performing his own works and some chamber music. He taught instrumentation and composition at the Leningrad Conservatory from 1937–1968, with brief breaks due to war and other political disruptions, and at the Moscow Conservatory in the 1940s. Since his death in 1975, Shostakovich has become one of the most performed twentieth century composers.

Birthday from *Children's Notebook for Piano*, Op. 69, No. 7 (composed 1944–45)
Among a huge output of symphonies, operas and chamber music, Shostakovich wrote only a few pieces for piano students. *Children's Notebook for Piano* was written for his eight-year-old daughter, Galina, for her studies on the instrument. The original set was published as six pieces. The seventh piece, "Birthday," written for Galina's ninth birthday in 1945, was added in a later edition.

Practice and Performance Tips
- The eighth note triplet staccato chords in measures 1, 3, 5, and later in measures 48–50, should be played with a crisp, buoyant bounce.
- After the introduction "fanfare," the music settles into a rather languid waltz in measure 7.
- Note that the right-hand melody is marked *cantabile* (singing tone) in measure 8.
- Beginning with measure 7, the left and right hands usually have independent and distinct articulation.

- Practice hands separately, paying carefully attention to the composer's slurs and staccato markings.
- In the left hand, in measures 7, 9–11 (and elsewhere), the implication is that after the first two slur notes, the quarter note on beat three is played with separation, though not a short staccato.
- In the right hand, in measures 9–10, the beat one quarter note should be played with separation, not slurred to the notes before or after it.
- Getting each hand's articulation independent and clear will take coordinate practice.
- Note that in measures 17–20 the right hand is playing phrases; the left-hand quarter notes should be played with separation, not slurred together.
- Divide the piece into sections for practice. Section 1: measures 1–; Section 2: measures 7–16; Section 3: measures 17–24; Section 4: measures 24–40; Section 4: measures 41–48; Section 5: measures 48–54.
- Shostakovich's composed articulations imply that he intended no sustaining pedal to be used in this piece.
- Do not forget the general festive spirit of celebration.

— Richard Walters, editor
*Joshua Parman, Charmaine Siagian
and Rachel Kelly, assistant editors*

Round Dance
from *For Children, Volume 1*

Béla Bartók

Fingerings are by the composer.

Ivan Sings
from *Adventures of Ivan*

Aram Khachaturian

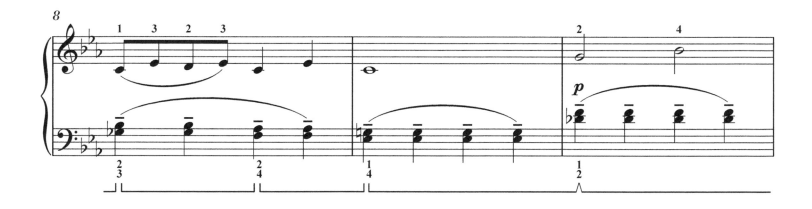

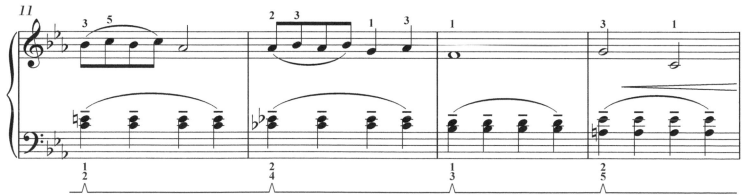

Fingerings are by the composer.

Slow Waltz
from *24 Pieces for Children*

Dmitri Kabalevsky
Op. 39, No. 23

Fingerings are editorial suggestions.

The Chase

from *30 Pieces for Children*

Dmitri Kabalevsky
Op. 27, No. 21

Fingerings are editorial suggestions.

Clowning
from *30 Pieces for Children*

Dmitri Kabalevsky
Op. 27, No. 10

Fingerings are editorial suggestions.

Festive Dance
from *Five Little Dances*

Paul Creston
Op. 24, No. 5

Fingerings are editorial suggestions.

Copyright, 1946, by G. Schirmer, Inc.
International Copyright Secured

Birthday
from *Children's Notebook for Piano*

Dmitri Shostakovich
Op. 69, No. 7

Fingerings are editorial suggestions.

Bagatelle No. 6
from *Fourteen Bagatelles*

Béla Bartók

Fingerings are editorial suggestions.

für mein nur Einziger Böski

Little Shimmy

George Antheil

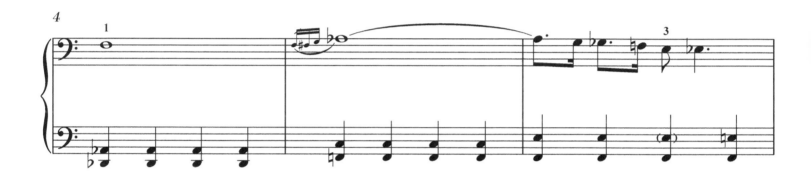

Fingerings are editorial suggestions.

Lyric Piece

from *30 Pieces for Children*

Dmitri Kabalevsky
Op. 27, No. 16

Fingerings are editorial suggestions.

Rustic Dance
from *Five Little Dances*

Paul Creston
Op. 24, No. 1

Heavily ♩ = 76

Fingerings are editorial suggestions.

Mountain Lullaby
from *Mountain Idylls*

Alan Hovhaness
Op. 119, No. 3

Fingerings are editorial suggestions.

Novelette
from *30 Pieces for Children*

Dmitri Kabalevsky
Op. 27, No. 25

Molto sostenuto [♩. = c. 56–60]

Fingerings are editorial suggestions.

to Number 220601

To My Steinway
from *Three Sketches for Pianoforte*

Samuel Barber

Fingerings are editorial suggestions.

to Jean
Petite Berceuse

Samuel Barber

Moderato con espressione [♩ = c. 76–80]

The fingerings in italics are Barber's.
Pedaling is editorial suggestion.

Regrets
from *Music for Children*

Sergei Prokofiev
Op. 65, No. 5

Fingerings are editorial suggestions.

Morning
from *Music for Children*

Sergei Prokofiev
Op. 65, No. 1

Andante tranquillo [♩ = c. 66–69]

[*with pedal*]

mf gravamente

Fingerings are editorial suggestions.

à Mademoiselle Jeanne Leleu

Prélude

Maurice Ravel

Assez lent et très expressif (d'un rythme libre) ♩ = 60 environ

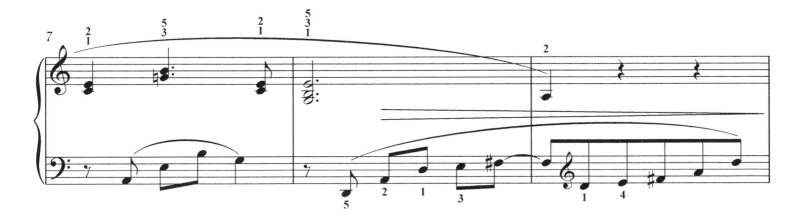

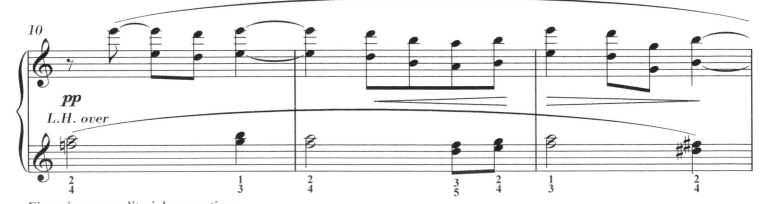

Fingerings are editorial suggestions.

Fable No. 9
from *Fables*

Robert Muczynski
Op. 21, No. 9

Fingerings are editorial suggestions.

Jeering Song
from *For Children*, Volume 1

Béla Bartók

Fingerings are by the composer.

A Little Prank

from *30 Pieces for Children*

Dmitri Kabalevsky
Op. 27, No. 13

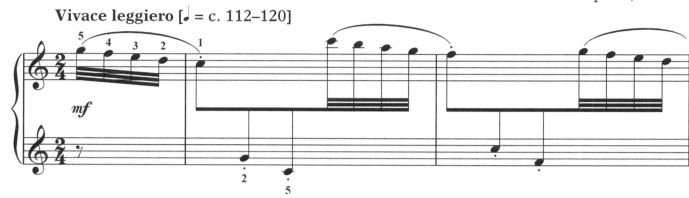

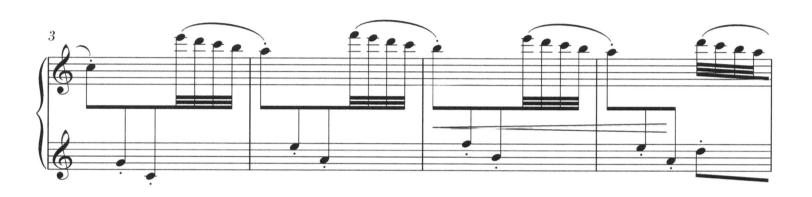

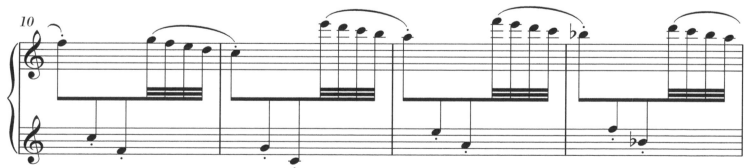

Fingerings are editorial suggestions.

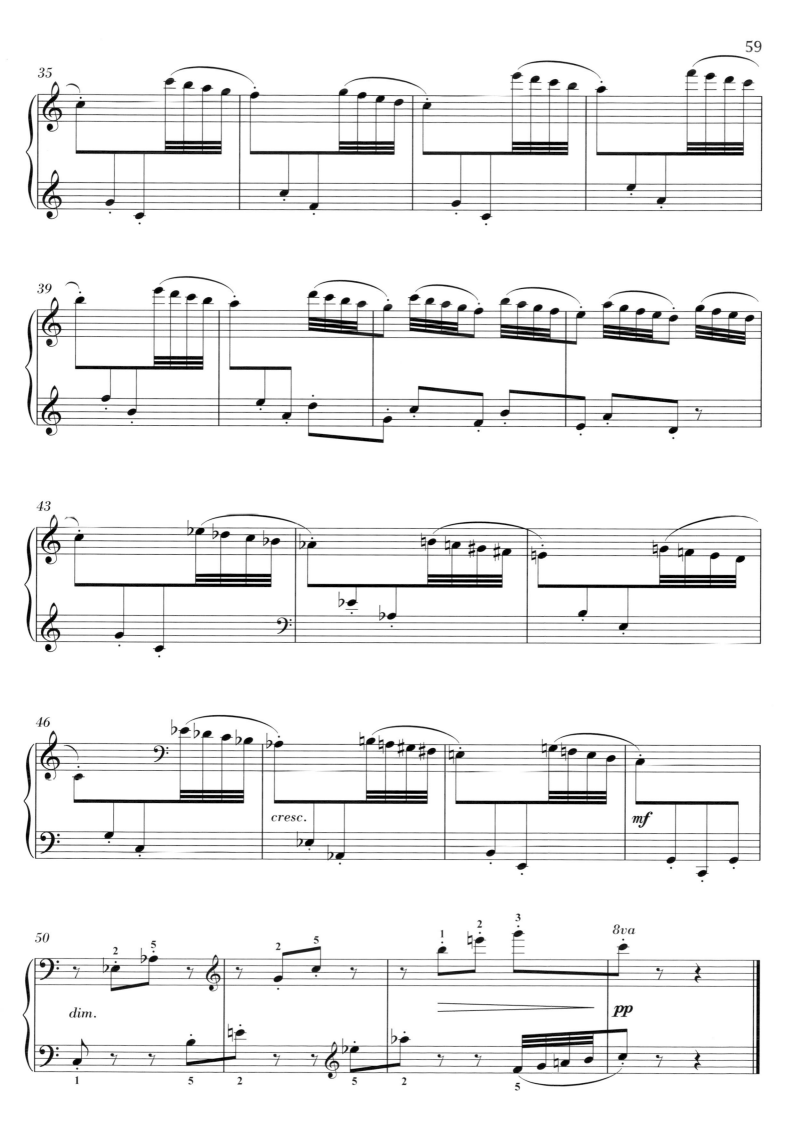

Playing Marbles
(Bolinhas de vidro)
from *Children's Festival: Little Suite for Piano*

Octavio Pinto

Allegro brillante [♩ = c. 96]

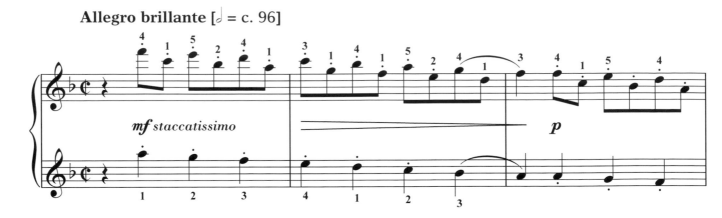

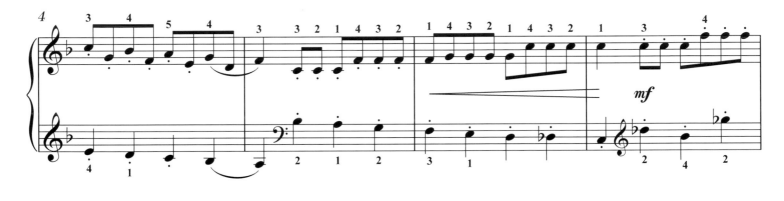

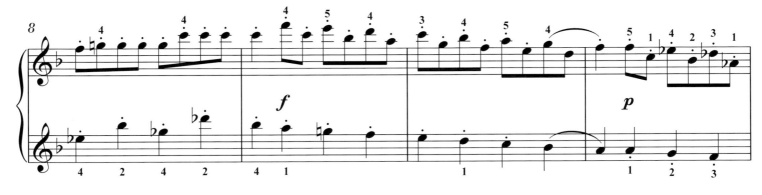

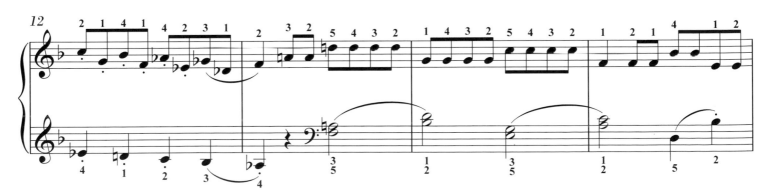

Fingerings are by the composer.

Prelude and Fugue in G Major

from *Six Preludes and Fugues*

Dmitri Kabalevsky
Op. 61, No. 1

Fingerings are by the composer.

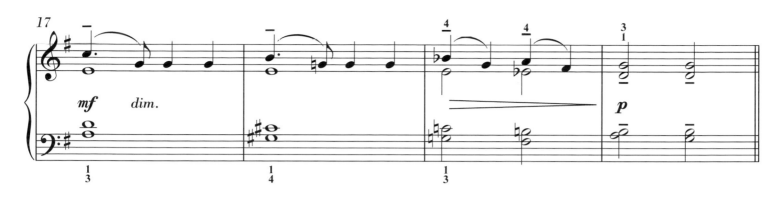

Poco più mosso

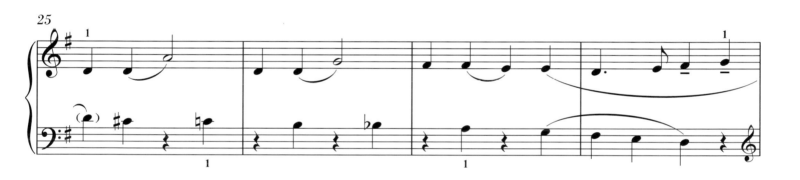

Promenade
from *Music for Children*

Sergei Prokofiev
Op. 65, No. 2

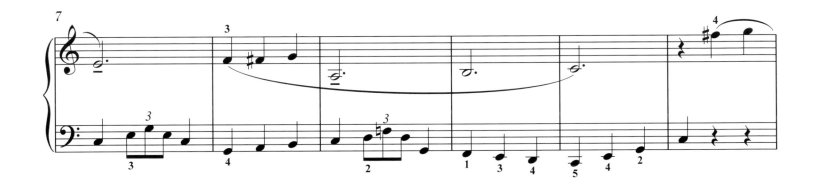

Fingerings are editorial suggestions.

Rondo-Toccata
from *Four Rondos*

Dmitri Kabalevsky
Op. 60, No. 4

Fingerings are by the composer.